I0234203

hades ladies

marnie heyn

The Writers' Bloc Press
1415 South State Street
Saint Joseph, Michigan 49085

Copyright © 1965, 1966, 1975, 1976, 2013 by Marnie Heyn

All rights reserved

Heyn, Marnie, 1949-
    hades ladies / by Marnie Heyn
      xx p. 25 cm.

ISBN 978-0-9883054-0-3
    1. Poems   2. Women's studies   3. Feminist
    literature   4. Formal verse   5. Spirituality
        I. Title

for my family

Parts of this manuscript received awards from the Hopwood Committee, which administers the Avery and Jule Hopwood Program at the University of Michigan.

ᏧᏫᏧᏫᏧᏫᏧᏫᏧᏫᏧᏫᏧᏫᏧᏫ

the swimmers surface

laps in lethe

the trees surround the lake

the swimmers surface

persephone reports in the underworld

persephone spreads
a copy of the daily news
out on a rock
and sits

one more year
one more harvest
she sighs
dirty nails
and getting pinched by
goatherds

she says
i have ceased to care
of your quarrel with my mother
there has been a change of regime
what with manure and irrigation

the old treaties are null
your lease on my life has
expired

my ankles are weak
and so
are my eyes
I am tired of being
a household plant

next year spring
may decline to
leave
may emigrate to some
more hospitable planet
pluto

Customs

Any of you who have never held
                a dear one's dirty shirt
secretly against your face, inhaled,
                and surpassed peace,
you are excused.
You may wander off along the banks,
or back the way you came.
So benighted in your innocence you are,
you have nothing to declare
and cannot cross the river.

The rest of us will sit on low pine pallets,
cheesecloth draped over us, our veils,
trying to forget the smell of band-aids,
and fire, wet soil, old cars,
impatiently waiting as eyes turn to splinters,
ears to leaves, skin to papery bark,
                tongue uprooted,
as the stubbornest sense is leached away
into the headwaters of Lethe.
Then we will be ready for the other side.

the high-backed canoe
for Rowan, before I knew you

In the high-backed canoe, baby is riding,
swept along under a translucent dome,
before the swell of a great spherical gong
struck with two hinged flails.
Ruddy billowing beasts
                    surge up in the shallows,
and ruffled creatures scrabble across the sky.
Densest crimson plush
                    makes chaise and canopy.
The rudder is clad with
                    huge curving sheets of nacre.
Cords of purple, brassy green and gold
                    slash through the hangings.
A pair of seven-stringed lyres
                    and an aeolian harp
are borne aloft.
The canoe grows smaller and smaller
as it approaches the shore
                    where attendants face upstream,
anxious to catch you as you dive headlong,
waiting to salvage
                    the unornamented ivory of the hull
of the canoe as best they can.

october

ropes shriek offstage as the sky scenes change
trees relinquish half their leaves
shift their grip to retain some
                        grasp on the upper world
cats on an orange crate
                        before a white wall in the sun
warm their paws in the drafts
exiles reconcile themselves
                        to new responsibilities
learn there are greater privations
than missing a favorite brand of tobacco
or a kind word every day

diptych: left panel
   prairie godmother

i have your picture
somewhere here
a thoughtless gift
that someone found
in a rack of humorous greeting cards
when i was young

you stand
in evaporating sepia twilight
before a sod cabin
one woman
with twelve or thirteen men
over the typeset legend
   Drop by any time!

the door frame gapes behind you
your lids and lips gape in your face
you stand like clothes on a hanger
depending toward the miser plain
not even weeds grew in your dooryard
frost and feet had scoured them away

i taped that picture inside my
red rubber notebook
and pondered it
between class bells
and with lunch
fruit pies made in iowa
and during saturday nights
i wondered why someone thought you funny

and why
i could still discern some home
in the socket of that hut
some light in the cavern of your eyes

and who did you ponder on winter nights?
the men who passed around you
a child not yet born or long since dead
a mother still living
in springfield or marion or camden
or buried since the latest blizzard
closed the prairie to news and riders

did you talk to the wind
or the blasted grain
or traders moving through
or the girl who once lived
in springfield or marion or camden
or did words fall away from your mouth
like your teeth?

your fingers were scarred with shocking corn
your lips withered with unanswered prayers
and unspent conversation
circumstance
necessity
turves
and rain buckets
flattened the angle
of your shoulders until
you were only a piece of prairie
standing on end

it no longer puzzles me
that you were the rooted one
while the bearded men around you
were poised for departure
even as the shutter dropped

falling east from denver
fleeing a man on the pacific brink
i rush toward the beacon and scent of chicago
between lincoln and sioux city
my radio pulls in signals
of buffalo hooves
and steam engines
the parching of salt swamps
women keening for starving braves
trappers paddling freezing rivers
panting mastodons
coyote panics
and countless padding feet
they all call through my antennae
and tell me
wait
but i do not hear you anywhere

if your picture does not lie
you could not have left so many
cousins with flashfrozen features
and only so many prospects
as stations on a dial

from the tools stacked outside your door
i know that you hoped for
a well in the dip behind the cabin

and a windmill on the nearest rise
a sloped roof for the winter
and even a chimney to draw the stovesmoke
but did you ever dream
the machines that would subdue the plains?

in the grocery store parking lot
i ask about sod huts
but everyone here has
aluminum sides now
your bones are mixed with sioux and buffalo
i would leave you some token
but i cannot find where you lie

diptych: right panel
                        gold star

you bought that dress new from the catalogue
in twenty-eight or twenty-nine
you were wearing it when your boy came home
on a forty-eight hour pass
in a khaki outfit
to say he was ordered to europe
and you were not to cry

he borrowed a brownie
from the fellow at the gas station
and dragged you
protesting
to face the sunlight
and hold very still
with starch in the hairs above your wrists
and fels naphtha drying on your knuckles
as he backed and filled
to bring your image into focus
he trimmed it to fit inside the gideon cover
and carried it in his blouse pocket

the silverwashed paper caught enough
your pride and your bewilderment
your tongue and gums in rictus
your rationed stockings
your crooked hips and shoulders
and your interrupted hands

he carried that picture right through v e day
with the note from the pastor
that you had died at christmas of pneumonia
until the jeep backed over him in france
in paris
and knocked the gideon away
onto the sidewalk
they missed it when
they took him away

some brooklyn boy found it
and kept it
and hawked it
after writing
        Take me – I'm yours!
under your peeling patent slippers
and making a thousand copies
to send to his buddies back stateside

likely he could not know
of the kids lying with you in a coaltown
graveyard
or the vfw star on the newest plot
of the plaque in the chapel
or the cost of false teeth
the medals still locked in the general store safe
or the fine truck garden going to seed

Tough cud
after Millay
for LB

   My dear, you would be like the camel
Which, exchanging New World for the Old,
Grew humped and glum, grew hooves of bone, and spits
Its food against its teeth to chew again,
Again, again. Stop gnawing on that septic
Transylvanian count, the Yanömamös'
Wife-theft wars and almond-fogged seraglios.
   Stop looking through your lashes. Take off
Those awful boots, and put your feet to carpet,
Grass, cement, and asphalt, tile and stone:
My dear, it is not *that* dreadful here.

the true confession of saint joan

i am sometimes sorry now
i did not have a child then
instead i
did battle

but true and good are the brides
of incubi
and of ideas
for we bear beautiful fruit

i wonder what she
will look
like

the frag man
          after Sappho

it is clear
now neither
honey nor the honey
bee is to be
mine again
since sense cannot follow
shockborne particles of gold and ebony
and sweet taste disperses like blood
like hope

demosthenes

lots of things are made that way
beaverboard
and the felt for mongol tents
and paper
nothing like so substantial
as the need that fashions them
except in some few cases

everything circles in
rock breaks rock
paper wraps rock
we toss pebbles in the dark
and know by the sea that we are within sound

the gospel according to someone else

hell's teeth
the worst of that place wasn't the cold
it was the smell
and that smug old man peering down

if it weren't for him i would have been
between linen sheets
in my parents' house
with a charcoal brazier
and the finest nurse
at hand
above the town of nasarot

but no
he had pretensions to royalty and
since the roads were clogged with snow
we couldn't take a cart
i bruised around on
the back of an ass
up and down the hills
to beit lohim
to register for the tax

and i went into labor then
and there
because that dull carpenter knew
he was cousin to a dead king
and was too sanctimonious to rent the bridal
suite
for me

you were someone else's first
he said
it's only for a night

but i was never like batshiva

so i dripped and heaved
alone
as it turned out
he slicked back his temples and brow
off to intrude on presumed relations
saying
women are supposed to know of these things

and i delivered
with an icy knife
and pink melted snow
myself

the old man stumped back into the shed
hauling a train of tourists
look at that
he said and
they said
amazing

i guess some of them felt
sorry for me
i was only fourteen
they loaded me up
with gift boxes
to cover up the dungsmell

to carry back to nasarot
and forget on a shelf
in my father's rich house

my first was a good boy
but the others were easier
the rusty carpenter took more to them
he thought they were more his
than my first
the old fool
i had to intercede between them
that is
until my oldest son's bar mitzvah
when my boy confounded the rabbis
with his learning
and his spirit
the carpenter saw the praise
heaped on the boy
and wanted it for his own
thereafter he treated our son as adopted
very graciously

my other children got along well
the boys were learned and hardworking
the girls gentle and hardworking
much gentler than i
the rounds of family
and house
and shop
kept me busy

mama and papa passed away
we sold their fine house

cleaning up i found
the presents of our midnight guests
that distant night in beit lohim
i showed them to yosiah
my moody oldest bachelor boy
all of thirty that spring

the oils and incenses
just made him more moody
that summer when the fig trees leafed
he went away
to solitude in high windy places
and teaching in temples in other towns

i said to him
be a rabbi here
in nasarot
and live at home
he just sighed
mama
the butcher calls me david's lamb
and laughs
no man is fully esteemed
in his own country
in his own house

nor i my son
nor i

so when i could
i followed him to other towns
up hill and down stream

his brothers and sisters sometimes came
to swell the multitudes
oh he denied me many times
but i brought him little comforts
mended his clothes
made him eat
those last three years

for me
his last week was
much harder than
his birth
the crowds throwing stones and sneers
dogs and jackals
i could not reach him
in his pain

his brothers fled
cowards
his sisters developed
vague female complaints
and the carpenter was deaf
when he chose to be
and shortly dead
without his will
but i stayed in yisrolayim
and was rewarded in my way

as he dragged the leafless treetrunk toward
golgotta
he stopped and straightened
turned to me
and called

brave daughter of channah
don't cry for me
but for yourself and
your other children
the day will come when
you will wish
you had been barren

he was wrong for
wisdom is justified
in her children
and i was left with nothing else

alone i pulled his body back in a cart
laid it in the tomb above nasarot
that holds the carpenter
and my other longdead kin

i went back to my other children
and my house
and birthing more grandchildren
i returned to my neglected study of the law
and tried to learn to write again
but my fingers were
so many withered twigs

and this pesach i am
again in yisrolayim
my children all dead
the house in nasarot burned
in the recent troubles
my care passes from grandchild to grandchild
no one notices what i wear any more

so i choose clothes of bright colors
and scamper through the market
on quiet sunny days
when the romans aren't about

but lately strange things come to me
lepers lurch from the shadows
        and beg me for ease
greedy urchins hide in my cloak
and silly girls clutch me and demand
i interpret their dreams
all folly

i thought you wanted the same
when you beckoned me in
and offered
a bit of cheese and olives
bread and wine

ah
if i were
other than i am
i could have been
a scholar or a prophet
but i was early sent
to be a mother
i wish it were enough
and i wish these ghouls
would stop plaguing me for mercy
from one who had never pitied me
and let me rest
and forget

you say your way goes north from here
well
mine goes south
a grinning granddaughter will trundle me
to sanctuary at masada
away from the ferment and rabble
good journey
and please help me stop
these rumors
if anyone asks
just say
that my boy was a good boy
if not always wise
and that i was once smart
and graceful
and proud
and even
at the end
not too willful or vain

Besoin
       for Lamarck

With leaching sight, dictating to his daughters
on his death bed, he fathomed nights
the like that Milton saw, and Blake:
Wish makes it so.

He saw a world organic to its core,
and we read the way life
has come in skeletal remains
which makes it so.

His thumbnail flicking fossils in the mines,
he knew wings without the thirst for flight
are no more than tattered, helpless hands:
Will makes it so.

When hunger drags us where we would not go,
or passion waits for times not yet in hand,
we must trust our need and our desire
will make it so.

noble portia at her window

something akin to plague
sweeps my world with
a broom of reeds
carrying the large
substantial
leaving the petty

it is only winter
leaves will not fall soon enough
to shelter me from the bright sun

civilization

i) driving a bad road in heavy traffic
    gritty
    worldweary i watch as
    a silent greybrown bird
    flies into the thicket of tires
    on the double trailer truck ahead
    and is flicked away onto the right shoulder
    a colorless papery scrap

   all day i have passed sad mammalian
   humps of castoff innertubes
   with a jolt of squeamishness for each
   but i have stopped for every hitchhiker
   a reserved flick of the eye *no knife no gun*
   nicely judged downshifting halts me
   just past the mouth of the onramp
   this car has no brakes
   no starter either so hitchhikers push
   my sweatshirt says *peace activist*
   my license plate says *outside agitator*
   but every town has a gas station with a phone
   from which my friends can hear me say
   it has broken down again wire cash

most places i've a friend with a couch or rug
  so i no longer wake rigid with cold
  inside my sleeping bag
  on a pew in an unheated sanctuary but
  i still think with morbid
              certainty or uncertainty
  of where my husband is what he is doing
  of my high school classmates
  who remember four war dead
  who bow their heads awkwardly
  while i am awkwardly upright
  who awkwardly deny a classmate
  imprisoned for draft refusal
  until the amnesty of another kid who grew up
  where a sandy river runs to the lake

ii) they have finally opened
    the last stretch of freeway
    and i drive north
    away from work
    the right direction at the wrong latitude
    two of us between bucket seat
                    and steering wheel
    you kicking and clawing to be free
    me hopelessly aching for rest

    as we cross the overpass
    i make my arrow click us into the left lane
    avoiding the patch where
    softpawed leviathans
    have pulled the paving blocks awry
    after we skid twice on black glare
    i spiral down to the old highway
    for now foxfire will warm us

    i trust you will come in your own time
    i know another way to go
    and when you are strong enough
    to come alongside me
    i'll trust my strength to take us home

ophelia on the job

Be more modest.
Lie down.
Roll over.
Play dead.
            – advice

he was somehow flawed
and could not love me
no matter
i earn my salt
my hands heft the spade that turns the earth

the man who held this job used to speculate
i simply rearrange the stack of clods
there is charm in the first few cuts
but by the time i have sunk to eye level
sloth or maybe husbandry has left unlit
the stars that i might see within this well
no matter

i can lie here
or dig to siam

antigone prays

at first in my infamous cave
i tried to sort out earth from stone
to pull air from the tempest

now i just ring
with my own heartheat
like all creatures
under the unseen sun

in this fading
i see the fabled lights
of the bear seekers
who have no need to lie

beautiful sisters of annam
oh avenge my brother
and bring my brother home

ଈ❧ଈ❧ଈ❧ଈ❧ଈ❧ଈ❧ଈ❧

laps in lethe

four quarter time
for Tom Bentsen 1952-1975

he played the bull fiddle
with his fingers instead of a bow
which was
for him
a daring act

he was an obliging kid who'd walk any number
of miles for rehearsal
his great fiddle straddling one hip
he was always on time
and he always said thank you for the ride home
after sitting alone in the back seat

my brother tells me that the last time the two of
them
played sweet ballads alternating sets with a
stripper
in an upper peninsula bar tom took great
delight
in chilling the nickels he tossed her under beer
mugs
he chilled them under so many mugs he forgot
and
had to dig out his seaman's papers to find the
name of his ship
to give my brother as an address
care of the *Edmund Fitzgerald*

the last time i saw him he had grown a broad
deep voice and a beard

he explained his study of great lakes navigation
rose from the wicker chair to point
down the road at lake michigan freighters
and said he aimed to steer an ore boat
when he had finished mariner's school

he realized his ambition
for the round earth's imagined corners
all lie on the bottom of jealous superior
and in his old folk music time
four four is one whole measure

postcard
  after a photograph by David Seymour

i tried to read your picture both ways
from the left as they still do
in the europe you fled
or abandoned
and from the right
as i was taught in a rusty little cheder
on a continent you never saw

it does not read to me
i stutter on the symbols
you wear
i think
a yarmulka and you stand
on ground littered with
fragments of clay or bone
there are so many

i learned to make my ches and kaph
but i cannot bend my tongue to the adoration
of the lace on your child's elaborate gown
washed clean of the needledrawn blood of its
maker
nor my speech conform to the shadow of a
bishop's crook
that creeps like a snail against your wall

power line and wristwatch
cannot disturb this chthonic scene
but you my brother
you bother me mightily
grinning in the shadow of the child you raise
proud of your sunblinded son's indifferent
onearmed benediction

maybe i hate you

i start up from sleep
in the room i dreamed of
long before i decided to move to this town
crushing weight of your body rolling onto me
unconscious in the dark persists
although it is full day

i run the tub
i must bathe before i go to work
months since and my sweat still smells of you
even the rapist who followed me
three weeks burlap bag in hand
could not reach where you have
scattered teeth of revenge
i prided once on not nurturing

i trusted my dreams once too

you would not as guest
why must you as invader

bonfire

the weather is mild
and kind friends
have adopted joe and me
and taken on our middleaged wedding
in a weekend already full
the new england neighborhood potluck
thanksgiving
their daughter in the homecoming queen's court
but they insist and we hike
across marshes and hills of wild cereals
i demonstrate grass sledding
i slide into a clammy little hollow
fine festering splinters from
                    achilles tendon to nape
where six charred logs
                    rest on a circle of black ash
and singed green shoots
                    bristle in the swampy ground

between knife and cracker
this is where epiphany strikes
as these enlightened people speak earnestly
and sip cocktails
i comprehend blasphemy
realize witchcraft and understand
                    who the holy office
dispatched

i do not remember their names
i do not remember what they knew

i was taught that
            my thumb tendons form a salt cellar
i was taught that
            epiphanies are part of adolescence
i flee across the terrace
and vomit on the dead roses
what is the omen from the fire last time?

lucy our hostess says *nerves*
puts her arm around my sobs
and sets me to stacking wafers on a tray
in the deserted kitchen where
departing guests come to wish me luck

when it is dark and i am calmer
we sit for dinner around a long plank table
warped under fat turkeys
                and centuries of bonhomie
lucy's daughter agnes
            in letter sweater and pleated skirt
gleams as bright as the pewter or brass

but i am not reconciled
the windows are still open this warm evening
distant chants make the screens thrum
and fires burn on the hills around the house

joe and carlo are pretending to hunt
while lucy and eight friends
                give me a bridal shower
their arms are full of gifts
                and their eyes of wishes

we sit on the brick hearth
i listen as they tell me about these objects

sources and histories
they lean above me
            with flames reflected on their faces

doctor teacher vet weaver herbalist
i am overcome with fear and a sense of loss
and run for the john
lucy asks *pregnant?*

i am angry
and helplessly silent

lucy and i have the house to ourselves
carlo has taken joe to a bar
a young man has taken agnes to the
homecoming dance
where she hopes to be crowned
she left moving carefully
rustling and scented
on her dyed pointed high heels

joe left looking disoriented
lucy and i sit on tall stools
me up to the elbows in hot soapy water
her with an orange dishtowel
and discuss our need for healing rituals
i want to know why all fertility festivals
                have become phallic
lucy reminds me of easter eggs

i am not satisfied
the impulse toward goddess of clay and straw is
gone

i sit on my four poster in an afghan
and nevertheless am chilled
by the meaning of bonfire

car tires ticking through gravel reminds me
of homecoming queen agnes and i realize
that this is how persephone was chosen
a tacit round of election and sacrifice

so when agnes comes in she finds me draped
and swaying on the stairs
i apologize to her and all her forerunners
for my lack of charity
        toward cheerleaders and prom queens
she is puzzled and faintly embarrassed
but i am able to sleep warmly til dawn

having made my peace with the world
i am ready to reassure joe
we set off in the sports car
he bought recently to replace his old truck
he says he got it to go with his new status
as respectable family man
that his truck was disreputable
but this new car is sedate and dignified

actually it looks racy and moves skittishly
and is altogether unlike him
he is so tender and reasoned and decent
i warm myself in his good regard
                    and a plaid lap robe
and find enough enjoyment
                    in the november sun
and the subtle colors of the coast in autumn

a cloud bank and the gas needle both threaten
joe turns trustingly for a peeling billboard
that promises gasoline and souvenirs
we enter a town that is
timbered and cobbled to the eyebrows
the filling station looks anachronistic
although it may have been here first

i plant the nozzle in the tank
joe puts up the car top
pays the man and comes back excited
he says i knew this was the place for you
see
a set of stocks ducking stool pond
and i drop the hose and run

my vision narrows
a tendon pulls in my left knee
my right ankle rolls awkwardly
i have never practiced running
but i seem to need to run now

joe's shoes clop after me
i want a bolt hole
an oak door dim shop startled clerk
a disciplined fire in a franklin stove

i brace myself against the door
but joe brushes the obstacle aside
and when he reaches for me

in my pain
i sink my teeth between his thumb and finger

i stand blanched and trembling
silently gnawing the only words i can remember
as joe explains my behavior
to a single dubious constable
as he buys a wrought-iron fireplace set
as he pays for all the gas i spilled
and keeps his bleeding hand out of sight
when we are on the road i tell him
i'm sorry i'm sorry it's me it's not you
and say at the reception
                    you'd better hold the knife
and i'll be the one to stand aside and guide it
and then he says listen
are you very sure
about this wedding?

The rightness of sky
after Richard Hugo's "The Standing Stones of
Callanish"

They told me, Flee them in snow,
                        under a full moon.
The shadows of these stones
                    will freeze you in yourself,
make you want to tell lies about
                    when you came here,
what it meant, what you cared about.
Still, you will stick to time and faith
like frost to the north pole.
You will sail on the lie of pattern,
the intoxication of pattern,
and try to snare birds to ride
instead of using your ears, wings of your mind.
Thankfully, you will fail.
Be gladdened by the honest changes of sea,
the shifts of wind that take
what needs to go: Do not make for grief
                        a special place.

If you are not meant to
                be here, your indifference
to stones will warn you away.
                    The truth of them
is this: When you belly up to a roomless wall,
touch the granite with your toes,
                        top rim of kneecap,
bony, grating crest of hip,
                springing base of ribcage bell,
inner surface of forearm,

heel of hand, clinging finger pads,
ear lobe, jaw, cheek,
          corner of mouth, rocking to brow –
when you touch each other, you trade skins.
Little changes.
Science can confirm contact,
          not the annealing of your soul.
Find a face your arms can span.
                    Rock the stone,
and you stir magma
          at your world's core, stars jingle
so far and fast the sound runs away from you
forever. The ones who shaped this place
shouted "Eh!" when they had finished.
They knew what it meant. They slapped
each other on their shoulder blades,
then wiped foam off
their lips onto the back of their wrists
and walked downhill,
carrying their lives like turtles.
The path lies there.

November eleventh

All deserts are manmade.
Scipio salted Carthage
Once, and now Sahara
Reaches toward Australia
And the pole. Green glass scars
Gobi and Mojave.
Japan's filled in a bay,
A dead Pacific patch.

A thin film of life makes
Some accommodation –
Brown plant, brown beast, brown lung –
While cynicism buffers
Alkaline barrenness,
But barrenness remains.
Blood lust brings us this far,
And never further on.

So I shall praise all these
Dull, negative virtues:
Patience, thrift, industry,
Meekness, sobriety.
Unshed tears make souls like
Rice paper, translucent.
Unstruck blows blossom from
Knuckles as fists unfurl.

nightmare

in the dark
in silence
alone in bed
i contemplate past triumphs
for reassurance in the night

when i see my first successes
i realize
i was not good
nor was i wise
i was merely anxious to please

eohippus

on the morning i had no one left to go to
nothing yet to accomplish
i filled a grocery bag with scraps
                    and bread crumbs
walked to the park
and staked out the bench
right across from the fountain

first come the pigeons
sinuous iridescent birds
that sing as sweet as any river
in zoos they would be marvelled at

i pitch pigeon feed to them
they eat

then the children come past
                    on their way to the playground
other people are with them
each child steps up on the curbing and drinks
turns away with a last mouthful
swallows
sighs and hops down
and runs away

at noon it gets crowded here with lunch people
but i put my bag up on the bench
and spread my hands and feet around
i know how to save my place
as well as anybody

Patience is one of those virtues
                              made of necessity

If you took the mottled thread
                    that holds the beads
that are the drops of water
                    falling on a forehead,
and the gristle that binds Chichevache's ribs,
and the hooked stick
                    that loops yarn over and over
through itself – solitary evenings in a chain –
and the reed that carries air
                    to the tortured lungs
of a fugitive hidden in bulrushes,
you could make a most unpalatable stew.
Penelope can have my share. You're welcome.

going on blue

phantom pain
is a consequence
of habituation
rather than real pathology

we can get accustomed
to the loss of sensation in a limb
the foot fallen asleep in a movie
on the other hand
i still miss the teeth i had pulled
first molars and wisdoms

there are all kinds of persistent pain
i know some people
they carry pain like a watch fob
and some carry it like a ball and chain
we all rush toward some anodyne

i am convinced
when i drive late at night
tired
that just beyond my headlights
there is a darker patch on the road
and if i could just get there fast enough
it would carry me
home

everyone i know
dreams of effortless flight

midwinter day
  for Don Hartwig 1950-1978

this year seasons were kind to me
heron flew about my shoulders
orange tree blossomed twice
warmth lingered into november

even on the shortest day i walked to work
following light down the river valley

walking away from you i turned the earth
puckered it between us
you who roared through the streets on a beetle
tattooing the sides and singing real loud
and me
and in each thaw
            i'll storm the dark ice with my feet
for you always

i'll choose to think
            somewhere you raise your eyes
to a high distant light
spreading smile across your face and rising
hands

something like a victory
for Hunyh Tan Mam, peacemaker

sisters and brothers
of the secretest part
of my heart

the sun is risen
beacon of bloodtinged fire
good guiding sister of all the stars
across the scarred and surging earth
across the blue vastness of space and time

the night of no moon is past
the mourning of no moon is past
the sun is risen
and we rise
and we plant
and we water
and we hope
but never do we wait agin
not until the harvest is one
and we are one

sisters and brothers who bring me the sun
i have never known a night so long
but it is over

the morning is at hand
the field is at hand
we will reap the hardwon harvest together
vietnam

Self-pity

I'm rigid on the bus at all the halts.
I set my jaw against sincere persuasion,
And that is not the gravest of my faults.

I overdress at any provocation.
My smile will never soothe a single sting.
I set my jaw against sincere persuasion.

I can't subtract. Above all things,
I dearly love to win an argument.
My smile will never soothe a single sting.

My correspondents don't get what I've sent.
I'm validated by the times I pine.
I dearly love to win an argument.

I decline my rightful turn in line
And trample on some hapless stranger's feet.
I'm validated by the times I pine.

I lead in polka dancing, miss the beat,
And trample on some hapless stranger's feet.
I'm rigid on the bus at all the halts,
And that is not the gravest of my faults.

clearly a fragment honey

i hack off my hair
like hindi women
to spite each man who dumps me

it has been a while
since it was all grown out
since i was twelve in fact
and played the lead in cinderella

time to grow it out again

when i was six of so
i had the recurring notion
that someone was trying to cut off
the space around my head
it was a painful notion

they call it penis envy

the coil

nance is bellyful of child
she carries her back like
diana's bow
she slides into the pool
for relief from the gravity

eldon carries more groceries now that
nance cannot hold them
he slumps around his larger burden
then reaches far back
to ease sacrificial muscles

my mother bends way down over a carton
of dusty bedtime stories
and resents
the effort of moving them
onto a shelf
although i do not think she grudges the work

my lover arches over me
and between dark and light
i see the trail of springing spines
that went into the making
cast up like eroded fish
on the shore of an
undated lake

thank you no

every time you call me princess
i smell sulphur

i know you have persuaded yourself
that you pay me a compliment
rub your knuckles on my fancy
but that is not the case

by choice i live in a century
that has disavowed slavery
the romance of royalty yanks on my hackles
i resent the pressure of the heel of your hand
on my breastbone
shoving me back into a past
littered with caste and rotten aspiration

that is why i snarl
when you call me lady
i'm assuming you know better than chicken
if you care to speak to me
call me by my name

in the belly

they wail
gestapo sirens here
why not?
the city council bought them cheap
war surplus
two dogs howl
in their pen next door
i would howl too
but the people i love
wear earphones
push the volume
seal all doors and windows
to be near major arteries
between the hurt
and the mender
between concentration camp
and resettlement center

Storing

If any of me is still here
        when harvest comes,
        I'll take the sixty holes
        that made my garden,
        set them together on the north face,
        and put pebbles in the bottoms

        for you,
        you.

Right here I'll make an ice cave.
        Now it's hot but
        I'll sprinkle well water
        at the end of it,
        my life.

        Ice.
        It will all be for you.

I want to come back here.
        That's why I do it.
        You're welcome.

I want to be around.
If my garden survives,
        I'll make it for you.

I'm saying,
        May all be well:
        So, I make it
        So.

thanksgiving

if the congresswomen had not gone
to indochina to tell the conquerors
who replaced their puppets who replaced
our puppets who ousted the prince

do not starve do not let
your people starve i could have
asked the indochinese who live in
my trailer camp *come for dinner*

my folks will be here then
i always make far too much
this was the first american holiday
but grief may overcome such welcome

as my forebears were thankful for
walking to the bus i see
them hugging their own lean trunks
like stroked mimosa watching film of

starved children flaccid as uprooted mimosa
walter cronkite groans
all children under the age of five will die
since i believe this my tongue

withers as glam's dark footprints fall
closer together here where they dump
corn on the ground i want
to tell my neighbors *save that*

rice for warmer weather the familiar
will not sustain you now eat
oats potatoes fatty meat oh someone
give squanto's simple gift to me

if i can speak if they
will come whatever goes before or
follows there will be a moment
that could properly be called grace

ৡৡৡৡৡৡৡৡ

the trees surround the lake

One thirty seven

In a strange land,
      I stood up by the river and dried my eyes.
I left my harp hanging
            in the midst of the willows,
For what holds me here holds others who say:
"I'm from Sion Heights, myself,
          and I sing hometown songs."
Why should I sing the old songs
          in this new land?
I could not forget them;
        my only fame as a singer
is in knowing all the words to all the songs,
And my only cunning is in making
          a bucket for the tunes.

I can give up the old songs, and sing;
        my chiefest joy is still anticipation.
If memory will not stretch to
        cover me today, let it go.
I will take what falls to me and raise it,
Raise it like a daughter or a new foundation.
My joy is no one's sorrow,
      no little ones dashed against rock.

belles balls

yesterday
afternoon
i took the children
and the cat
and ate grass
it is something i do whenever
i am on the ground
i eat grass like any cow or sheep
in this special kind of fall
this last rise of summer grass
life retreats to the roots
i pick out only dry
brownbottom blades
no tender firm meat or
sweet tasteless sap
and i think of my life
and i think how true

lying in the bath
at the intersection of
my body and the tile wall
at the oneway intersection of liberty and state
in the surface of water
we chomp
and the last blade i
plucked out had
life still
succulent
bright
green
thick   juicy   base

and i laughed and bit
and thought
how true

the old stone

the cobalt train of day
sweeps down the western sky
toward my source
and washes your skin to
bluemilk marble
opens your eyes and veins to lapis
leisurely brushes the fringe of gold
across your brow
then lengthens the hem of darkness

and i sorrow for
the age of stones
that flowed like the sea
that flowed like ink
when knives were made of wood
and locks of ribbon
when you and i had futures
lost in legend

then lamps on
and specs on
elemental harmonies are gone
we burn away the remnants of
a former life
and sleep
cloaked in green

antigone
murmurs in my dreams

horror story

they have marked me out
from the rest of my kind
the poisonous and irritating sorts
wasps
mosquitoes ignore me like a backdrop

but buffalo treehopper burrows under the knob
of my wrist
to lay her eggs
vanessa atalanta
smudged underside blue eye-spot
extends coiled tubular tongue to eat
having tasted my forearm
with her stunted forelegs
brown miller batters my armpits and nape

even red-faced wren
clasps my deltoid
and eyes my crown

cherry bark

across the street
when i was small
was a garden
saved for times like spring
and mom is at the store

a cherry tree grew there
touchstone for twilight games of tag
but lonely enough in daylight
to tolerate my climbing
impudence

since then
plaster casts
watermarked papers
bagels after ballet
glinting oil landscapes

flash me back to touch her bark
the rough shiny skin of an orchard widow
corseted in motheaten snow
and flushed by tickling fingers

whistle me back within my senses
mudknee corduroys and two sweaters
time in my hands
and paleflower twigs plaiting light in my mind

the rod of jesse

every may
the same old story
jake walks around the corner
of the house
braces his ladder
against my middle
and knocks all my blossoms to the ground
they look like tardy snow
he rakes them away and dumps them
in the far corner of the garden
with old carrot tops and
cat litter
he only wants to prevent
wanton apples on his lawn

in June he peels up my skirts
snips off any dangling twig or
straggling branch
he only wants to keep
his picture window tidy
and allow more sun in the playroom
but i live on my leaves
and losing the bottom margin hurts

and then in July
back jake comes with the ladder
to yank off the three infant apples
hidden above his presumed reach
he always finds them
and takes them
though

he only wants to prevent
dawn starling noise
but if i have no fruit
i have no winged visitors
around the edge of
that hill
over there
i get glimpses of
my matronly cousins
they peek and wave but
they go on about
their own lives
they think i
am idle

late in august i turn brown
prematurely
jake could have seen
he was killing me
but he just brings out more
sprays and prunes
i wish he would catch on
i do not know how long
i can keep
this up

spa

shouldered aside by granite and limestone
by magma and impervious basalt
ozarks water rushes through a gap in the
ancient bruised stone

all the diamonds buried here
are long since dissolved
in hard water
that mixes their carbon
with iron and calcium
that flushes frail people
feeds sturdy plants
and breathtaking cold lakes

this is another kind of election
both water from a tap
and water through a sieve
are thrust like poor alms up from the bedrock
patient supplication of a recurrent star

my brother aspires to sleep in these mountains
to walk through rising mist and falling rain
to savor his whiskey and take long showers
and ponder the lessons outside his door

i heard your arabesque
in passing
pulled off the road
to smell your hot spring
impatience sprouts
from my shoulders
like wings
but you are still here
i guess
so am i

mustard

ground and mixed with hot water
yields a mild fragrant sauce

with cold liquid the flour
creates the familiar ting and smack
of hot dog

with two slices of ice and lettuce would make
a sandwich of fire

seen properly is
the shortest straightest line from
french to chinese food
saffron leaping from a bed of green

crucible of pneumonia
cold comfort of royal foodtaster
currency of faith

sativa variety deft enough to distinguish
between tilled and waste ground
makes seeds with the flax and
soup greens amongst the weeds

seen properly this hard small sphere is
the shortest straightest line from me to you

persephone and the chickweed

a seed is sprouting
inside my ribs
watered by bitter melon springs

the snow shadows are melting
i have ambitions
to fly in sunlight

your voice rises
and my waxsealed
wingspan melts
and fails
and falls

your anger makes me plummet
reason drops away
extremities grow numb
old wounds tear open

but i soar lie a vine
and cauterize all the
old wounds
and sing under ether
and slip back

secondhand anger pinches
like pride
but quick
before you see
i turn

my points inward
and sheathe
my knives

when you flare
the old sharpness
reemerges
old callouses and elbows
folding under
chicken wings

frightened children fold their hands and worlds
press together
dreams of
making wine
from visions of flight

for a fact
cowards who love
grow cringing
grow
heedless

the snow shadows sink earthward
i have ambitions
to fly in sunlight

graft

you see *he says* to make a dwarf
we need two trees
one larger root
one smaller top
we make matching notches
cuts and slices
and then we mate
the male base and the flowering female part

my uncle guides me through
his plant nursery
assumes a nurturing voice
sows ideas left and right with his blacknailed
hands
we stroll out through the fruit trees and
he shows me

he grapples giant metal shears
chews through bark and grain and pith
slides a bright knife between long fibers
gouges out vacuums with a pointed little awl
he does this twice
once to each of two young trees
then grind the ends together to make them fit
he seals the gaps and cracks with salve
wraps the union with sapsmelling tape
rocks back on his haunches
and says
wahlah

i am appalled
i ask him
what do you do with the leftover parts?

he says compost
and waves my disgust away like flies
he says if we join the smaller root with the
larger top
the fruiting branch overbalances
and pulls the join apart
the effort is wasted

i ask can you not save many parts
mate smaller cherry to apricot
and larger plum with apple?

he wags his head
kicks the woodscraps away and says
those matches never conform
to proper shape
and the fruit always tastes
unnatural

i ask can you not join two trees
stand them together
make them intertwine
without destroying
a good part
of each?

he strangles me about the waist
throws me in the air
he laughs and says tender baby
we could only do that on a bushelsize planet
or a world turned inside out

here
he hands me
eat a pear

the old witch curses

my body
gnarled and harvested
sits by the fire in a broom chair
that holds a chill far too well
and never warms in summer

i lullaby the soup
sing it stories i wish were true
nasty things i wish i had said
alas
my only audience is the soup
i stir it with a wild green song
pepper it with the hearts of cruel lovers
onion it with sweet blizzards

once i gathered magic herbs across the fields
but now my feet stumble
my eyes confuse the leaves
i cannot remember which groves are sacred
and which merely useful
so i sit while my other stirs
young hungry fields
and ripens like a grain head
wind combed
sun tossed

while i sit with dried thyme and the spoon
darkened and hardened as no one will hear
my heart's with a shadow that moves through
the night

go dark windwraith
go
wander well

punkin

i may be always far away
and since it seems to follow
a night for all souls
i send you this gift
a handful of soapy flat almondeye seeds
which will grow
anywhere
like mustard
and are as faithful
to their kind

no cicadas this september

iron filing sparrows
rush into the trees
above the bus stop
squabbling like relatives
at a pauper's funeral

perhaps the relatives are actually excited heirs
perhaps the pauper was a generous spendthrift

i may have the story all wrong
the birds could be reciting or inventing
fabulous avian realms far to the south
where the coming superlative flinty cold
                              will not penetrate
where swarms of savory nutritious insects are
for the snapping and swallowing

they may believe that
somewhere toward the sun i take on faith
cicadas sing their rusty songs
all day

the wooden flute

my father cut the birches down
the summer that i moved away
the trees were diagnosed as beetled
dying

my mother wrote
dad tried to make a bench
of their stumps and boards but
the wood splintered and snapped
no use

so dad broke the birches to chunks
to stop doors steady trash cans
chock tires and fasten the cold frame
but not to burn

birch burns readily
but dad is tender
toward the bugs
when i visit
i notice my fine trees scattered
like a spiteful puzzle

last sunday i sat alone
in the tired café he introduced me to
the flautist wheezed toward midnight

in a sudden energetic phrase i heard again
the lake wind
birch leaves sighing
scarlet
before dusk shades them to grey

i dance for the birches
and they are gone

In praise of John Chapman

Apple seeds are my caviar among
                    all bright, sweet seeds.
Pomegranate seeds are friable and wonderful.
I love the seeds of all dark grapes,
Of both the round, black sort
                    with the tough, bitter skin,
And the oval, russet sort with skin
                    that tears like my own.
The seeds of figs delight me;
          I fight birds over sunflower seeds.
I have great esteem for watermelon seeds,
   the white for eating and the black for spitting.
The seeds of berries are joyous on my tongue.
The tucked velvet seed of a peach is
                    a joy to my tongue and lips.
Cherry seeds are sleek and amiable;
                    so also are citrus seeds.
The seed of a date is a marvel cleft for me.
An elusive pleasure is the tomato seed,
                    in mouth and in earth.
Avocado seeds and I nod in passing;
                    pear seeds are all right.
Prune seeds are tolerable, except in danish.
I can respect an olive seed,
                    unless the can is mislabeled
And thereby I have fractured a tooth or two.
I can even muster a sneaking affection
                         for the pepper seeds
That sidle between my teeth and burn my gums
While I try to look couth with my
                    fingers stuck in my mouth.

But when I consider you, pomme d'oeil,
Tin pot on head, book sprawled on knee in your
afternoon slumber,
Or lacing the hills with your feet
While your right hand does its own
                  dance with the seed bag,
Plunge, fling; plunge, fling;
Then I am grateful beyond measure
                        for a bounty
Rarer than the roe of salmon,
    for the apple seeds that are my caviar.

tonic

take
for fever of soul
or season

fill a pot
with lemon balm
hyssop
and jamaica flower

observe the liquid silver of
a walker evans photograph

add verbena
fennel seed
a bit of cinchona
and peruvian wood

seek out a small vista of sidereal time

now willow bark
valerian
patient cuckold
and wild plum

tie your hair back from your shoulders
juniper berry
balsam wood
chamomile
and tansy
add
and cover with fresh spring water

then when the sun drowns in the trees
dress in finest linen
lie on a bed of blue spruce boughs
take this mixture
and drink
then stir
gently

ৡৡৡৡৡৡৡৡৡ

Marnie Heyn is a scholar of languages and history, a fierce gardener, and her hometown's market fiddler.

www.ingramcontent.com/pod-product-compliance
Lightning Source LLC
LaVergne TN
LVHW061220060426
835508LV00014B/1371